HIP-HOP & R&B

Culture, Music & Storytelling

DJ Khaled

HIP-HOP & R&B

Culture, Music & Storytelling

Beyoncé

Bruno Mars

Cardi B

Chance the Rapper

DJ Khaled

Drake

Jay-Z

Pharrell

Pitbull

Rihanna

The Weeknd

MASON CREST

Joe L. Morgan

HIP-HOP & R&B

DJ Khaled

C Storytelling

Mason Crest
450 Parkway Drive, Suite D
Broomall, Pennsylvania 19008
(866) MCP-BOOK (toll free)

First printing
9 8 7 6 5 4 3 2 1

ISBN (hardback) 978-1-4222-4187-5
ISBN (series) 978-1-4222-4176-9
ISBN (ebook) 978-1-4222-7629-7

Library of Congress Cataloging-in-Publication Data

Names: Morgan, Joe L. author.
Title: DJ Khaled / Joe L. Morgan.
Description: Broomall, PA : Mason Crest, 2018. | Series: Hip-hop & R&B: culture, music & storytelling.
Identifiers: LCCN 2018020770 (print) | LCCN 2018021053 (ebook) | ISBN 9781422276297 (eBook) | ISBN 9781422241875 (hardback) | ISBN 9781422241769 (series)
Subjects: LCSH: DJ Khaled--Juvenile literature. | Sound recording executives and producers--United States--Biography--Juvenile literature. | Rap musicians--United States--Biography--Juvenile literature.
Classification: LCC ML3930.D59 (ebook) | LCC ML3930.D59 M67 2018 (print) | DDC 782.421649092 [B] --dc23
LC record available at https://lccn.loc.gov/2018020770

Developed and Produced by National Highlights, Inc.
Editor: Susan Uttendorfsky
Interior and cover design: Annalisa Gumbrecht, Studio Gumbrecht
Production: Michelle Luke

QR CODES AND LINKS TO THIRD-PARTY CONTENT

CONTENTS

KEY ICONS TO LOOK FOR:

Words to understand: These words with their easy-to-understand definitions will increase the reader's understanding of the text while building vocabulary skills.

Sidebars: This boxed material within the main text allows readers to build knowledge, gain insights, explore possibilities, and broaden their perspectives by weaving together additional information to provide realistic and holistic perspectives.

Educational videos: Readers can view videos by scanning our QR codes, providing them with additional educational content to supplement the text. Examples include news coverage, moments in history, speeches, iconic sports moments, and much more!

Text-dependent questions: These questions send the reader back to the text for more careful attention to the evidence presented there.

Research projects: Readers are pointed toward areas of further inquiry connected to each chapter. Suggestions are provided for projects that encourage deeper research and analysis.

Series of glossary of key terms: This back-of-the-book glossary contains terminology used throughout this series. Words found here increase the reader's ability to read and comprehend higher-level books and articles in this field.

DJ Khaled
HIP-HOP & R&B

Chapter 1:

Highlights of DJ Khaled's Career

DJ Khaled has produced ten albums in a career that has been active since 2006. Two of his albums debuted at number one on the *Billboard* 200 Chart. His most successful effort to date, the 2016 release of MAJOR KEYS, received a Grammy nomination for Best Rap Album and reached certified Platinum status by the Recording Industry Association of America (RIAA), an accomplishment earned for selling 1 million albums or more.

DJ Khaled has been and is a larger-than-life figure in the hip-hop world. Highlighted throughout this chapter are noteworthy moments, singles, and top album downloads that have shaped his career into what it is today.

DJ Khaled's Playlist

LISTENNN ... THE ALBUM
(Released June 06, 2006)

DJ Khaled released his debut album through Terror Squad Entertainment and Koch Records months before his thirty-first birthday. The seventeen-song offering sold 40,000 copies in its first release week and reached the number twelve position on *Billboard*'s Top 200 Chart. The album helped establish a spot for DJ Khaled among hip-hop's up-and-coming new stars and featured collaborations with a who's who list of stars, including John Legend, Kanye West, Young Jeezy, Rick Ross, Pitbull, Trick Daddy, Akon, Fat Joe, Dre, and Lil Wayne. The lead single, *Holla at Me*, was released three months before the album, on February 28, 2006. DJ Khaled has continued to use this marketing technique of releasing lead singles before an album to boost interest and fan anticipation.

Collaborations

- *Born-N-Raised*, featuring Pitbull, Trick Daddy, and Rick Ross
- *Gangsta* _____, featuring Young Jeezy, Bun B, Slick Pulla, and Blood Raw
- *Grammy Family*, featuring Kanye West, Consequence, and John Legend
- *Problem*, featuring Beanie Sigel and Jadakiss
- *Holla at Me,* featuring Lil Wayne, Paul Wall, Fat Joe, Rick Ross, and Pitbull
- *Addicted*, featuring Juelz Santana
- *Watch Out,* featuring Akon, Styles P, Fat Joe, and Rick Ross
- *Destroy You*, featuring Krayzie Bone and Twista
- *Never Be Nothing Like Me*, featuring Lil Scrappy and Homebwoi
- *Candy Paint*, featuring Slim Thug, Trina, and Chamillionaire

Scan the code here to listen to listen to *Grammy Family*, one of the big-name collaborative singles from DJ Khaled's debut album, Listennn ... the Album

- *MIA*, featuring Lil Wayne
- *Where You At*, featuring Freeway and Clipse
- *Still Fly,* featuring Birdman and Chop
- *Dip Slide Ride Out*, featuring T.I., Big Kuntry King, and Young Dro
- *Movement*, featuring Dre
- *The Future of Dade,* featuring Brisco, Dirty Red, Dela, Lunch Money, Co from Picacalo, Hennessy, and P.M.

WE THE BEST
(Released June 12, 2007)

DJ Khaled's second album debuted at number eight on the *Billboard* 200 Chart and received mixed critical acclaim. Fans seemed to like it, though, as 79,000 copies were sold the first week. The twelve-song sophomore offering was preceded by the single *We Takin' Over*, released March 27, 2007, roughly two-and-a-half months before WE THE BEST'S release. The single reached numbers twenty-six and twenty-eight, respectively, on *Billboard*'s Hot R&B/ Hip-Hop Songs and Hot 100 Charts.

Collaborations

- *Intro (We the Best)*, featuring Rick Ross
- *The Movement (Skit)*, featuring K. Foxx
- *We Takin' Over*, featuring Akon, T.I., Rick Ross, Fat Joe, Birdman, and Lil Wayne

Scan the code here to listen to listen to *We Takin' Over*, the first single from DJ Khaled's second album, WE THE BEST

- *Brown Paper Bag*, featuring Dre, Young Jeezy, Juelz Santana, Fat Joe, Rick Ross, and Lil Wayne
- *I'm So Hood*, featuring T-Pain, Trick Daddy, Rick Ross, and Plies
- *Before the Solution*, featuring Beanie Sigel and Pooh Bear
- *I'm from the Ghetto*, featuring Dre, The Game, Jadakiss, and Trick Daddy
- *Hit 'Em Up*, featuring Bun B and Paul Wall
- *"S" on My Chest*, featuring Birdman and Lil Wayne
- _____ *I'm from Dade County*, featuring Dre, Trick Daddy, Trina, Rick Ross, Brisco, Flo Rida, and C-Ride
- *The Originators*, featuring Bone Thugs-n-Harmony
- *New York Is Back*, featuring Ja Rule, Fat Joe, and Jadakiss

WE GLOBAL
(Released September 16, 2008)

The third album release from DJ Khaled came on his newly formed We the Best Music Group label, together with Koch Records, on September 16, 2008. The lead single, *Out Here Grindin*, was released four months earlier, on May 05, 2008, and features vocals by Akon, Rick Ross, Lil Boosie, Trick Daddy, Ace Hood, and Plies. The album, which debuted at number seven on the *Billboard* 200 Chart, features collaborations with a host of rap and hip-hop artists. In addition to the musicians listed on the lead single, The Game, T-Pain, Bun B, Nas, Kanye West, Fabolous, Fat Joe, Sean Paul, Busta Rhymes, Pitbull, Casely, and Flo Rida also participated on the production.

Collaborations

- *Standing on the Mountain Top*, featuring Pooh Bear and Ace Hood
- *Go Hard*, featuring Kanye West and T-Pain
- *Out Here Grindin*, featuring Akon, Rick Ross, Young Jeezy, Plies, Lil Boosie, Ace Hood, and Trick Daddy
- *Go Ahead*, featuring Fabolous, Lloyd, Rick Ross, Flo Rida, and Fat Joe
- *I'm On*, featuring Nas
- *Red Light*, featuring Game
- *We Global*, featuring Trey Songz, Fat Joe, and Ray J
- *She's Fine*, featuring Sean Paul, Missy Elliott, and Busta Rhymes
- *Final Warning*, featuring Rock City, Bun B, Blood Raw, Ace Hood, Brisco, Bali, Lil Scrappy, and Shawty Lo
- _____ *the Other Side*, featuring Trick Daddy and The Dunk Ryders

Scan the code here to listen to listen to *Out Here Grindin*, a collaborative single from DJ Khaled's third album release, WE GLOBAL

- *Bullet*, featuring Rick Ross and Baby Cham
- *Blood Money*, featuring Brisco, Rick Ross, Ace Hood, and Birdman
- *Defend Dade*, featuring Casely and Pitbull

VICTORY
(Released March 02, 2010)

The fourth album from DJ Khaled debuted at number fourteen on *Billboard*'s 200 Chart, sold 28,000 copies in the first week, and was proclaimed by AllMusic.com reviewer David Jeffries as a "fist-pumping song cycle of triumph in the hood." It was released through We the Best Music Group and E1 Records on March 02, 2010, and featured several collaborative efforts, including the singles *Fed Up* (featuring Usher, Young Jeezy, Rick Ross, and Drake) and *Put Your Hands Up* (featuring Schife, Young Jeezy, Rick Ross, and Plies). The second single released, *All I Do Is Win*, with T- Pain and Ludacris, was the album's most successful track. It was certified triple Platinum by the RIAA.RIAA (the Recording Industry Association of America's Certification Program).

Collaborations

- *Intro*, featuring Diddy and Busta Rhymes
- *All I Do Is Win*, featuring T-Pain, Ludacris, Rick Ross, and Snoop Dogg
- *Put Your Hands Up*, featuring Young Jeezy, Plies, Rick Ross, and Schife

- *Fed Up*, featuring Usher, Young Jeezy, Rick Ross, Drake, and Lil Wayne
- *Victory*, featuring Nas and John Legend
- *Ball*, featuring Jim Jones and Schife
- *Rockin' All My Chains On*, featuring Bun B, Birdman, and Soulja Boy
- *Killing Me*, featuring Buju Banton, Busta Rhymes, and Bounty Killer
- *Bringing Real Rap Back*, featuring Rum
- *Bring the Money Out*, featuring Nelly, Lil Boosie, Ace Hood, and Schife
- *On My Way*, featuring Kevin Cossom, Bali, Ace Hood, Ball Greezy, Iceberg, Desloc, Gunplay, Rum, and Young Cash
- *Rep My City*, featuring Pitbull and Jarvis

WE THE BEST FOREVER
(Released July 19, 2011)

DJ Khaled's fifth album, WE THE BEST FOREVER, was released on July 19, 2011. The twelve-track offering was the first album in his career that was released by a major recording label, Universal Motown Records, and it included participation by We the Best Music Group, Young Money Entertainment, and Cash Money Records. It debuted in the number five position on the *Billboard* 200, with more than 53,000 copies sold its first week. The lead single, *Welcome to My Hood*, features Rick Ross, Plies, Lil Wayne, and T-Pain.

Rick Ross

Collaborations

- *I'm on One*, featuring Drake, Rick Ross, and Lil Wayne

- *Welcome to My Hood*, featuring Rick Ross, Plies, Lil Wayne, and T-Pain

- *Money*, featuring Jeezy and Ludacris

- *I'm Thuggin*, featuring Waka Flocka and Ace Hood

- *It Ain't Over Til It's Over*, featuring Mary J. Blige, Fabolous, and Jadakiss

- *Legendary*, featuring Chris Brown, Keyshia Cole, and Ne-Yo

- *Sleep When I'm Gone*, featuring The Game, Busta Rhymes, and CeeLo

- *Can't Stop*, featuring Birdman and T-Pain

- *Future*, featuring Ace Hood, Meek Mill, Big Sean, Wale, and Vado

- *My Life*, featuring Akon and B.o.B.

- *A Million Lights*, featuring Tyga, Mack Maine, Cory Gunz, Jae Millz, and Kevin Rudolf

- *Welcome to My Hood (Remix)*, featuring T-Pain, Ludacris, Busta Rhymes, Twista, Mavado, Birdman, Ace Hood, The Game, Fat Joe, Jadakiss Bun B, and Waka Flocka

Scan the code here to listen to listen to *I'm on One*, DJ Khaled's collaboration with Drake, Rick Ross, and Lil Wayne from the album WE THE BEST FOREVER

Kiss the Ring
(Released August 21, 2012)

DJ Khaled began work on his sixth album, Kiss the Ring, in 2011, releasing this twelve-song effort on August 21, 2012, though the label Universal Republic Records, together with We the Best Music Group and Cash Money Records. The recording debuted at number four on the *Billboard* 200 Chart, selling 41,000 copies in its first week. The album featured collaborations with a list of hip-hop stars (see below), and the lead single, *Take It to the Head*—which features Chris Brown, Rick Ross, Nicki Minaj, and Lil Wayne—was another teaser that was released four months before the album, on April 03, 2012.

Collaborations

- *Shout Out to the Real*, featuring Meek Mill, Ace Hood, and Plies
- _____ *& Bottles (Let's Get It Started)*, featuring Lil Wayne, T.I., and Future
- *I Wish You Would*, featuring Kanye West and Rick Ross
- *Take It to the Head*, featuring Chris Brown, Rick Ross, Nicki Minaj, and Lil Wayne
- *They Ready*, featuring J. Cole, Big K.R.I.T., and Kendrick Lamar

Scan the code here to listen to listen to *I Did It for My Dawgz*, one of the promotional singles from DJ Khaled's sixth album, Kiss the Ring

Scan the code here
to listen to listen to
No New Friends
from DJ Khaled's
seventh release,
SUFFERING FROM SUCCESS

- *I'm So Blessed*, featuring Big Sean, Wiz Khalifa, Ace Hood, and T-Pain
- *Hip Hop*, featuring Scarface, Nas, and DJ Premier
- *I Did It for My Dawgz*, featuring Rick Ross, Meek Mill, French Montana, and Jadakiss
- *I Don't See 'Em*, featuring Birdman, Ace Hood, and 2 Chainz
- *Don't Pay 4 It*, featuring Wale, Tyga, Mack Maine, and Kirko Bangz
- *Suicidal Thoughts*, featuring Mavado
- *Outro (They Don't Want War)*, featuring Ace Hood

SUFFERING FROM SUCCESS
(Released October 22, 2013)

The seventh release from DJ Khaled appeared on October 22, 2013, this time through Universal Music Group's division Republic Records, along with DJ Khaled's We the Best Music Group and Cash Money Records, owned by Birdman. The musician titled this album SUFFERING FROM SUCCESS after a doctor's visit to treat a bald spot in his beard. The doctor told him it was related to the stress of his job and that he was literally suffering from his success! The fourteen-track album featured collaborations with many hip-hop stars and hit the number seven spot on the *Billboard* 200 Chart in its first week, with 27,000 copies sold.

Collaborations

- *Suffering from Success*, featuring Future and Ace Hood
- *I Feel Like Pac/I Feel Like Biggie*, featuring Rick Ross, Meek Mill, T.I., Swizz Beatz, and Puff Daddy
- *You Don't Want These Problems*, featuring Big Sean, Rick Ross, French Montana, 2 Chainz, Meek Mill, Ace Hood, and Timbaland
- *Blackball*, featuring Future, Plies, and Ace Hood
- *No Motive,* featuring Lil Wayne
- *I'm Still*, featuring Chris Brown, Wale, Wiz Khalifa, and Ace Hood
- *I Wanna Be with You*, featuring Nicki Minaj, Rick Ross, and Future
- *No New Friends*, featuring Drake, Rick Ross, and Lil Wayne
- *Give It All to Me*, featuring Mavado and Nicki Minaj
- *Hells Kitchen*, featuring J. Cole and Bas
- *Never Surrender*, featuring Scarface, Jadakiss, Meek Mill, Akon, John Legend, and Anthony Hamilton
- *Murcielago (Doors Go Up)*, featuring Birdman and Meek Mill
- *Black Ghost*, featuring Vado

Puff Daddy

I Changed a Lot
(Released October 23, 2015)

I Changed a Lot is the eighth album release from DJ Khaled, released on October 23, 2015. It sold 25,000 copies—referred to as equivalent album units due to its digital release—and debuted at number twelve on the *Billboard* 200 Chart. We the Best Music Group was again involved in its production, and it was released through RED Distribution. The single *They Don't Love You No More* was released as a teaser an amazing eighteen months before the album, on April 29, 2014.

Collaborations

- *I Don't Play about My Paper*, featuring Future and Rick Ross

- *I Ride*, featuring Boosie Badazz, Future, Rick Ross, and Jeezy

- *Gold Slugs*, featuring Chris Brown, August Alsina, and Fetty Wap

- *I Swear I Never Tell Another Soul*, featuring Future, Yo Gotti, and Trick Daddy

- *I Lied*, featuring French Montana, Meek Mill, Beanie Sigel, and Jadakiss

- *How Many Times*, featuring Chris Brown, Lil Wayne, and Big Sean

- *You Mine*, featuring Trey Songz, Jeremih, and Future

- *Every Time We Come Around*, featuring French Montana, Jadakiss, Ace Hood, and Vado

- *I Ain't Worried*, featuring Ace Hood and Rick Ross

- *They Don't Love You No More*, featuring Jay-Z, Meek Mill, Rick Ross, and French Montana

- *My League*, performed by Mavado

- *Hold You Down,* featuring Chris Brown, August Alsina, Future, and Jeremih

- *Most High*, featuring John Legend

MAJOR KEY
(Released July 29, 2016)

DJ Khaled released his ninth album, MAJOR KEY, through We the Best Music Group and Epic Records on July 29, 2016. By November of that year, the release was certified Gold by the RIAA. A production must sell 500,000 copies in order to be certified Gold. The lead single, *For Free*, was released on June 03, 2016, only six weeks before the album.

This work represents DJ Khaled's most recognized production to date, earning a Grammy nomination for Best Rap Album. The release debuted in the number one position on the *Billboard* 200 Chart and helped further establish his "cred" among hip-hop's best artists.

Scan the code here to listen to listen to *I Got the Keys* from DJ Khaled's ninth album release, MAJOR KEY

Collaborations

- *I Got the Keys,* featuring Jay-Z and Future
- *For Free*, featuring Drake
- *Nas Album Done*, featuring Nas
- *Holy Key*, featuring Big Sean, Kendrick Lamar, and Betty Wright
- *Jermaine's Interlude*, featuring J. Cole
- *Ima Be Alright*, featuring Bryson Tiller and Future
- *Do You Mind*, featuring Nicki Minaj, Chris Brown, August Alsina, Jeremih, Future, and Rick Ross
- *Pick These Hoes Apart*, featuring Kodak Black, Jeezy, and French Montana
- _____ *Up the Club*, featuring Future, Rick Ross, YG, and Yo Gotti
- *Work for It*, featuring Big Sean, Gucci Mane, and 2 Chainz
- *Don't Ever Play Yourself*, featuring Jadakiss, Fabolous, Fat Joe, Busta Rhymes, and Kent Jones
- *Tourist*, featuring Travis Scott and Lil Wayne
- *Forgive Me Father*, featuring Meghan Trainor, Wiz Khalifa, and Wale
- *Progress*, performed by Mavado

Nicki Minaj

GRATEFUL
(Released June 23, 2017)

GRATEFUL is the tenth album released by DJ Khaled. Released through Epic Records and We the

Best Music Group, it debuted at number one on the *Billboard* 200 Chart. The album was certified Gold by Canada's Music Canada and Denmark's IFPI Denmark services and Platinum in the United States by the RIAA. The lead single *Shining* was released a few months early, on February 12, 2017. Another single, *I'm the One*, debuted at number one on the *Billboard* Hot 100 Chart and became DJ Khaled's first number one single.

Interestingly, DJ Khaled's son, Asahd, is named as the album's executive producer. The proud father said he could tell if the songs were going to be successful by the baby's reaction to them. Asahd has his own attorney to handle the royalties and other business matters associated with the album.

Collaborations

- *(Intro) I'm So Grateful,* featuring Sizzla
- *Shining*, featuring Beyoncé and Jay-Z
- *To the Max*, featuring Drake
- *Wild Thoughts*, featuring Rihanna and Bryson Tiller
- *I'm the One*, featuring Justin Bieber, Quavo, Chance the Rapper, and Lil Wayne
- *On Everything*, featuring Travis Scott, Rick Ross, and Big Sean
- *It's Secured*, featuring Nas and Travis Scott
- *Nobody*, featuring Alicia Keys and Nicki Minaj

Scan the code here to listen to listen to *Shining*, a collaborative single from DJ Khaled's tenth album, GRATEFUL

- *I Love You So Much*, featuring Chance the Rapper
- *Don't Quit*, with Calvin Harris, featuring Travis Scott and Jeremih
- *I Can't Even Lie*, featuring Future and Nicki Minaj
- *Down for Life*, featuring PartyNextDoor, Future, Travis Scott, Rick Ross, and Kodak Black
- *Major Bag Alert*, featuring Migos
- *Good Man*, featuring Pusha T and Jadakiss
- *Billy Ocean*, featuring Fat Joe and Raekwon
- *Pull a Caper*, featuring Kodak Black, Gucci Mane, and Rick Ross
- *That Range Rover Came with Steps*, featuring Future and Yo Gotti
- *Iced Out My Arms*, featuring Future, Migos, 21 Savage, and T.I.
- *Whatever*, featuring Future, Young Thug, Rick Ross, and 2 Chainz

Jadakiss

DJ Khaled's Performances and Appearances

This impressive artist appeared on stage for a surprise performance along with Chance the Rapper at the 2017 iHeartRadio Music Festival held in Las Vegas, Nevada, on September 23. He also performed alongside singers Demi Lovato and Rihanna, Quavo, and a host of other stars on the festival's closing day.

DJ Khaled has performed live on the road multiple times since 2012. Some of his memorable shows include a performance at the BB&T Center in Fort Lauderdale, Florida, on June 12, 2014, at 103.5's The Beat Down Concert. Trey Songz, Future, and Kendrick Lamar also appeared.

Meek Mill's concert at the Wells Fargo Center in Philadelphia, Pennsylvania, March 21, 2015, featured DJ Khaled, along with Yo Gotti, Rick Ross, and Jadakiss.

Other concerts that DJ Khaled has performed at include Nas's concert on November 07, 2015, at the USF Sun Dome in Tampa, Florida. Nas, Fabolous, Yo Gotti, Jim Jones, Lil Wayne, August Alsina, iLoveMakonnen, Cyhi Da Prynce, Troy Ave, Tink, Famous Kid Brick, Trae Tha Truth, and Shy Glizzy appeared during that occasion as well.

At the Hot 97 Summer Jam, June 05, 2016, DJ Khaled performed at New Jersey's MetLife Stadium in East Rutherford with Big Sean, Pusha T, A$AP Rocky, A$AP Ferg, Bryson Tiller, Young Thug, Tinashe, Kid Ink, Future, Travis Scott, and Terror Squad (DJ Khaled's initial group, more in Chapter 2).

Beyoncé's *Formation* Tour

DJ Khaled was especially thrilled to open for Beyoncé during the North American leg of her *Formation* Tour. The tour began April 27, 2016, and was based on her Grammy- and Peabody-Award–winning album LEMONADE. Starting in DJ Khaled's home city of Miami, it continued through thirty-two

Scan here to watch DJ Khaled's performance alongside Demi Lovato, Quavo, and other stars at the 2017 IHeartRadio Music Festival in Las Vegas, NV, September 23, 2017

concert dates and ended on October 07, 2016, at the MetLife Stadium in East Rutherford, New Jersey.

DJ Khaled opened twenty-two of the tour's thirty-two North American shows, including the opening concert in Miami and the closing show in East Rutherford.

2018 Demi x Khaled World Tour

DJ Khaled is scheduled to join up with singer Demi Lovato on their 2018 Demi x Khaled World Tour. The North American performances to promote Demi's album, TELL ME YOU LOVE ME, began on New Year's Eve, December 31, 2017, in Miami Beach, Florida, at the music venue LIV at Fontainebleau. The tour is scheduled to extend through March 31, 2018, ending at Amalie Arena in Tampa, Florida.

Demi Lovato

Collaborating and Performing with Other Artists

This musician is essentially a producer, whose albums continually feature some of rap's top-name celebrities. He doesn't rap, but he does appear on tracks, often shouting his famous catchphrase "We the Best!"

Nearly all of DJ Khaled's tracks on his ten album releases were collaborations with artists across the spectrum of musical genres. He says that his relationships with other artists have grown as their individual careers have flourished, and now they are in a position to help each other out on various projects. For instance, the all-star effort *I'm the One*, appearing on his GRATEFUL album through We the Best/Def Jam/Epic Records, featured the talents of Chance the Rapper, Quavo, Justin Bieber, and Lil Wayne. The track was DJ Khaled's first to debut at number one on the *Billboard* Hot 100 Chart, and it was also only the fifth song since 2015 to debut at number one. Adding to the accolades, it was the first hip-hop/rap song to hit number one since Eminem's *Not Afraid* in 2010.

Chance the Rapper

The collaboration, co-written by DJ Khaled and released on April 28, 2017, first appeared as a single that he initially teased on Instagram. The song has achieved Platinum status in fifteen countries, including the UK, United States, and Canada.

V.S.O.P. by PNC, featuring DJ Khaled and David Dallas
(Released June 02, 2009)

One collaboration by DJ Khaled was with Australian rapper PNC on his second studio album release, BAZOOKA KID. The song *V.S.O.P.* is the sixth track on the album, but it was not released as a single. It featured DJ Khaled and David Dallas.

Way Too Cold by Kanye West, featuring DJ Khaled
(Released April 17, 2012)

Another collaboration for DJ Khaled is Kanye West's single *Way Too Cold*, which was initially titled *Theraflu*. DJ Khaled is heard as the record's front man, and the song was prominent in Kanye's 2012 WATCH THE THRONE Tour.

On the way to one of the tour's shows on April 27, 2013, DJ Khaled's tour bus caught fire! Although no lives were lost, the blaze did destroy about $500,000 in DJ Khaled's personal items, including jewelry and clothing. He tweeted about the incident, saying,

"lockerz.com/s/204681889 I'm sry I couldn't make it 2 grad bash it was out my control my tour bus caught on. . . http://m.tmi.me/p21di"

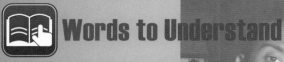

Words to Understand

deejay (DJ): a slang term for a person who spins vinyl records on a turntable; aka a disc jockey.

emigrate: the act of leaving your country of birth to live as a resident in another country.

immigrant: a person holding legal or nonlegal status in a country who has come from another country.

legendary: something known as being great, or historically memorable.

mogul: someone considered to be very important, powerful, and in charge; a term usually associated with heads of businesses in the television, movie studio, or recording industries.

Chapter 2

Starting in the United States

Growing Up

DJ Khaled was born on November 26, 1975, in New Orleans, Louisiana, under the birth name of Khaled Mohamed Khaled. His parents lived in Palestine as young adults. His mother grew up in the city of Ramallah, located in the central West Bank, and his father was raised in a city nine miles away, called Al-Mazra'a ash-Sharqiya. They **emigrated** to the United States in their mid-20s, just before DJ Khaled was born. He is pretty tight-lipped about his parents—who they are and what they are doing—but you can find pictures of him online with his family from time to time.

DJ Khaled is a U.S. citizen, being born and raised in the United States, even though his parents, who are still alive, are foreign-born **immigrants**. He has a brother, Alla Khaled, who is known in acting circles as Alec Ledd. He has made a name for himself in several Disney projects *(Hannah Montana, The Suite Life on Deck)*, as

Ramallah is a Palestinian city in the central West Bank located 10 km north of Jerusalem. On the left is a minaret of a mosque.

well as by making guest appearances on television shows such as *The Division, Charmed,* and *Crossing Jordan.*

DJ Khaled's parents are also musicians and were a large influence in developing his early love and appreciation for music and hip-hop. During his early years, DJ Khaled held a job at Odyssey Records, formerly located on Canal Street in the famous French Quarter district of New Orleans. The record store was a meeting place for musicians, budding hip-hop artists, and **deejays**. It is where DJ Khaled met Cash Money **mogul** and owner, Birdman, and fellow New Orleanian, Lil Wayne.

When DJ Khaled turned twenty-three, he made his way to Miami, where he spent time co-hosting a radio show on Miami's WEDR 99 Jamz 99.1 FM called *The Luke Show*, with 2 Live Crew's **legendary** front man Luke Campbell. He also spent time deejaying, hosting his own show on WEDR in 2003.

During the early stages of his career in music, DJ Khaled went by a variety of names, including Arab Attack, Beat Novacane, Big Dog Pitbull, The Don Dada, Mr. Miami, and Terror Squadian. The name "Arab Attack" was meant to describe the way he attacked music as a deejay. After the September 11, 2001, attacks on New York City; Shanksville, Pennsylvania; and the Pentagon, in Arlington, Virginia; DJ Khaled stopped using it as a show of respect for the men and women killed in the terrorist attack.

Working with Lil Wayne

Lil Wayne appeared on his first DJ Khaled track in 2005: *Holla at Me*, from DJ Khaled's first album, LISTENNN. . . THE ALBUM. That lead single also features Rick Ross, Paul Wall, and Pitbull. At the time, Lil Wayne was a member of Birdman's Cash Money Records. He was taken under Birdman's wing, and Birdman also helped DJ Khaled develop into the star he is today.

In an interview with *DJ Booth*, DJ Khaled stated that he wanted Lil Wayne on *Holla at Me* "cause that's my brother and he's one of my favorite rappers." Since 2005, Lil Wayne has appeared on every album DJ Khaled has released.

The two artists have maintained a close personal and professional relationship into adulthood. For instance, Lil Wayne joined him at a nightclub in Miami on December 10, 2017, to help DJ Khaled celebrate his forty-second birthday.

Fast Fact 1:

The young artist got his start as a performer in 2005 when rapper Fat Joe convinced an executive at a major label to take on the up-and-coming rapper. At the time, DJ Khaled was known mostly for his skills as a deejay, and his excitement and energy was described by Fat Joe as having "a Fat Joe on steroids."

Expanding Family

DJ Khaled used the social media platform Snapchat to announce that he and his longtime girlfriend and fiancée, Nicole Tuck (who is also a Palestinian-American), gave birth to their first child on October 23, 2016. The couple named their son Asahd Tuck Khaled.

DJ Khaled and Nicole first began dating sometime around 2011 when he took an ownership interest in a clothing company named ABU Apparel, owned by Nicole. She

Nicole Tuck, DJ Khaled, and Asahd Tuck Khaled at the 2017 MTV Video Music Awards held at the Forum in Inglewood, CA, on August 27, 2017

holds a 2003 bachelor's degree in fine arts from Marymount Manhattan College and a master's degree in education from New York's Fordham University. She has served as an unofficial business representative and manager for the artist and is one of the steadiest influences in his life.

Musical Progress

It was mentioned that DJ Khaled got his start in hip-hop through the efforts of Fat Joe, the head of Terror Squad Entertainment Group, in 2005. (See the section on Terror Squad later in this chapter.) It was DJ Khaled's connection to Cash Money owner, Birdman, and his relationship with a group of young stars that propelled him to stardom. That crowd includes Lil Wayne, with whom he has released several collaborative tracks since coming on the scene in 2006.

DJ Khaled was actively honing his craft as a deejay and entertainer as early as his preteen years in New Orleans. He went from working at Odyssey Records to getting involved in deejaying at

Fat Joe at the 2017 iHeartRadio Music Awards held at the Forum in Inglewood, CA, on March 05, 2017

local clubs and parties. He used these opportunities to develop his skills and further convince himself that his future career was in music.

DJ Khaled's formal education ended after high school when he graduated from Dr. Phillips High School in Orlando, Florida. His music education continued to grow, first as a prodigy of Birdman and Luke Skywalker, then later of Fat Joe, just prior to the release of his first album in 2006. The education he received after school from his mentors has proven to be as valuable, if not more so, in helping him become the successful artist that he is today.

Becoming a Star

Nine singles from DJ Khaled's albums have been certified Platinum by RIAA since his first release. In addition, seven other singles have been certified Gold, and one album has reached Gold status and another album has reached Platinum.

His initial release, LISTENNN. . . THE ALBUM, rose to number twelve on the *Billboard* 200 Chart, as mentioned in Chapter 1. Since that 2006 release, his achievements include reaching the *Billboard* charts with a number one single, three top ten hits, and twenty-six total landings for various singles on the *Billboard* Top 100 Chart.

Terror Squad

In addition to his successful career as a deejay and music collaborator, DJ Khaled is also a former member of a collective group that goes by the name Terror Squad. The group was founded in 1992 in New York City by rapper Fat Joe, who assisted DJ Khaled in becoming a hip-hop artist in his own right. The group grew into the record label Terror Squad Entertainment Group, which was initially distributed by Atlantic Records and is now under E1 Music.

Lil Wayne

Terror Squad Entertainment Group served as the label for many of DJ Khaled's early albums, including his first release in 2006, LISTENNN . . . THE ALBUM. His early career releases as part of Fat Joe's Terror Squad Entertainment Group were distributed through Koch Records, which later became E1 Records. Then DJ Khaled formed his We the Best Music Group label in 2008, and from his third album to his tenth, he has used that label for every album. Along the way, he's also worked with Birdman's Cash Money

Records, Lil Wayne's Young Money Entertainment, Universal Motown and Universal Republic Records, and Jay-Z's Roc Nation LLC, which currently represents DJ Khaled as an artist.

Text-Dependent Questions:

❶ What hip-hop star, also born in New Orleans, is a childhood friend of DJ Khaled?

❷ What one name did DJ Khaled initially use as an early performer? What was the reason he stopped using the name?

❸ What city did DJ Khaled and his family move to in 1998 to further his music career? With what famous rapper did he co-host a radio show?

Research Project:

DJ Khaled, whose full name is Khaled Mohamed Khaled, was born in the United States in the city of New Orleans, Louisiana, on November 26, 1975. His parents, who are Palestinians and Arabic musicians of their own, emigrated to the United States during the 1970s to escape civil war and growing tension between Palestinians and the emerging state of Israel, and to provide better opportunities for their family.

Palestinian-Americans make up roughly 10 percent of the 2 million Arab-American community in the United States. Although Arab-Americans in general and Palestinian-Americans specifically make up a small part of the population, they have made significant contributions to the field of entertainment. Perform a little research and list five famous Arab-American performers (can be musicians, actors, authors, or athletes), and mention any significant accomplishment for which they are known.

A&R: an abbreviation that stands for Artists and Repertoire, which is a record company department responsible for the recruitment and development of talent; similar to a talent scout for sports.

handle: a slang term for a person's name.

resides: where a person lives.

tidbits: pieces or a portion of a whole; a term usually associated with "bits" of advice given or provided.

dogged: persevering in effort; tenacious; marked by stubborn determination.

Social Media Presence

DJ Khaled has not only established himself as a mogul in the music industry, he is also making his way into related areas. This includes social media, and specifically Snapchat, a platform that was created on July 08, 2011, under its original name "Picaboo." The platform differs from the more commonly used Facebook and Twitter because it is based solely on the use of multimedia images (such as photos and video, known as "snaps").

The deejay became an avid user of Snapchat, and as his career began to rise, so did his popularity—and the popularity of that social media platform. He has been labeled the "King of Snapchat" by Coca-Cola's senior vice president of content Emmanuel Seuge. DJ Khaled's snaps average 3 to 4 million views each, making DJ Khaled's the most popular on Snapchat.

He uses his Snapchat account to announce events and happenings, and everything associated with his label We the Best. His **handle** on his @KhaledSnapchat account is @djkhaled305. The number "305" is a reference to the area code of Miami, Florida, where he currently **resides**—just like Pitbull's alias, Mr. 305.

In addition, he has more than 3.4 million Facebook and 3.9 million Twitter followers. This has given DJ Khaled wide appeal and a huge audience for his music. He promotes his comings and goings via all his social media accounts: Facebook (https://www.facebook.com/officialdjkhaled/), Twitter (@djkhaled), and Instagram (@djkhaled), where he has 8.9 million followers.

Streaming Availability

DJ Khaled's music is available for streaming on all of the major music-streaming and internet radio services. The list includes Spotify, iTunes, Apple Music, Pandora, and Google Music, as well as channels available on Last.fm, Slacker Radio, and iHeartRadio. A simple search of the name "DJ Khaled" will put you in touch with any one of the countless tracks he has recorded during his career, which has spanned more than a decade so far! You can also find information on his upcoming tours and entertainment news.

Apple Music

The artist signed a deal with Apple in February 2016 to host a weekly show under his recording label We the Best, and a biweekly television series available through Apple TV and for download on Apple's iTunes. The deal was an attempt to leverage DJ Khaled's success on Snapchat in hopes of creating new Apple Music followers.

Award-Winning Deejay

In his career to date, DJ Khaled has been nominated for forty-eight awards and has been the recipient of seventeen, all since 2007. This recognition has given a formal nod to his musical talent and recognizes what he has contributed to hip-hop since first breaking on the scene in 2006.

Here is a listing of the awards DJ Khaled has won during in his career:

American Music Awards

Favorite Rap/Hip-Hop Song—*I'm the One*, featuring Justin Bieber, Chance the Rapper, Quavo, and Lil Wayne | Won in 2017

BET Hip-Hop Awards

Best Collaboration—*I'm So Hood (Remix),* featuring Young Jeezy, Ludacris, Busta Rhymes, Big Boi, Lil Wayne, Fat Joe, Birdman, and Rick Ross | Won in 2008

MVP of the Year | Won in 2009, 2015, and 2017

DJ of the Year | Won in 2009, 2011, 2012, 2015, and 2017

Hustler of the Year | Won in 2015

Best Collabo, Duo or Group—*Wild Thoughts*, featuring Rihanna and Bryson Tiller | Won in 2017

Ozone Awards

Best Radio DJ | Won in 2007

Best Video—*We Takin' Over*, featuring Akon, T.I., Rick Ross, Fat Joe, Birdman, and Lil Wayne | Won in 2007

DJ of the Year | Won in 2008

Soul Train Music Awards

Best Collaboration—*Wild Thoughts*, featuring Rihanna and Bryson Tiller | Won in 2017

Teen Choice Awards

Choice R&B/Hip-Hop Song—*I'm the One*, featuring Justin Bieber, Chance the Rapper, Quavo, and Lil Wayne | Won in 2017

The Keys

On November 22, 2016, DJ Khaled published his first book, titled *The Keys*. It was published by Penguin-Random House affiliate Crown Archetype and is 224 pages in length. The topic is motivational content based on his "keys" to life, to his success, and small gems of knowledge he has picked up along the way.

The information is a collection of his personal philosophies, which have been collected over his lifetime, compiled, and released in book form. It is appropriate for all audiences, young and old.

Harvard University School of Business

Professor Anita Elberse invited DJ Khaled to speak to her students in 2016. He covered topics of the business of entertainment, media, and sports in the class on December 11. The visit was sponsored in conjunction with DJ Khaled's work with the nonprofit program Get Schooled, an effort to encourage teens and young adults to graduate from high school as well as attend college.

In keeping with the way he operates, DJ Khaled videoed the talk for his Snapchat page, which he shared with his online fans. He also shared the following **tidbits** of wisdom with the students who attended and sat in a packed auditorium.

" *What's so beautiful about life is that it's an experience and I want to let people know, if you ever fall, all you have to do is just get up and keep moving forward, you know what I'm saying? It's about teaching the young world not to fall. Giving them the keys so they won't fall …*

If you want to be a teacher, whatever you want to do, do it. There's no reason why you couldn't do it. We blessed. We got life so we can accomplish anything we want to accomplish. **99**

2017 NPR Interview

DJ Khaled sat down with NPR's David Greene in a January 06, 2017, interview to discuss his recently released book, *The Keys*. During the interview, the new author spent time explaining what his keys are and how they can be used to inspire his fans—particularly youth—to find their own keys. Here are tidbits of quotes explaining his views as he sat down in the discussion with David.

On the question of what the keys mean to him:

99*Well "the keys" man, is the keys to success, keys to life—you know what I'm saying?—keys of winning, keys of joy, keys of happiness. The keys never run out, you know? Each key leads to the next key.*

. . . that's how the book is, you know what I'm saying? Because when I was coming up in the game and growing up, they hid the keys from me.

. . . they are the people that don't want me to do this interview with you, you know, they. . . .They come in so many different forms, but they are the people that we need to stay away from, you know what I'm saying? And honestly, I had somebody actually come up to me and say, Khaled, you will be nothing. You're just a DJ. You're going to be local forever. You're not going to be able to succeed. But I stayed focused. I didn't listen to them. **99**

On what advice he would give to those up-and-coming artists who are looking to establish themselves:

... this book is definitely to uplift the young world because, you know, we just have different ways of saying it. I was just doing an interview earlier, and I was like, you know, our moms and dads always taught us, you know, to do great things, you know what I'm saying? We bless that family, but sometimes you've got to get somebody to translate it in a different way, you know what I'm saying?

One of the motivating factors that keeps DJ Khaled driven on a path to success is his **dogged** persistence, even in the face of adversity. This became evident in 2015 when he decided to visit his friend, rapper Rick Ross, at Ross's Miami home via a jet ski. On the way back to his own house, DJ Khaled became disoriented and lost while riding his jet ski along in the Atlantic Ocean.

Maintaining his composure, he recorded the event to his Snapchat page, repeating one of his keys to success to his online fans: "The key is to make it."

He made it home, but not before crashing the Snapchat platform with more than 3 million views of his "perseverance at sea" snap.

Scan here to view DJ Khaled's famous Snapchat video of being lost at sea while returning to his Miami home from December 2015

Hard Work Pays Off

DJ Khaled's success has come not only through his collaborations and deejaying but also as a producer, **A&R** rep, and label head. He owes his success to being in the right place at the right time and working hard at developing skills. His efforts have been paid in full through the recognition that he has received and the awards he has won so far in his career.

DJ Khaled has realized success despite his untraditional path to stardom. He is a rarity in that he is one of the few true deejays who has been able to release albums, collaborate with top stars and recording artists—like Jay-Z and Beyoncé—and use a little-known social media platform as a launchpad to promote and energize a fan base that has propelled him to greatness.

Beyoncé

Text-Dependent Questions:

❶ How many music awards has DJ Khaled been nominated for? How many awards has he won?

❷ How many times has DJ Khaled won BET's Hip-Hop DJ of the Year?

❸ What is the name of the book DJ Khaled wrote in 2016?

Research Project:

DJ Khaled has multiple awards nominations and wins from the American Music Awards, BET, and others, including two Grammy Award nominations. The recognition he has received as an artist has been hard fought and not without those insisting that his craft, deejaying, was not in the same class as that of traditional performers, like singers and rappers. DJ Khaled documented the drive and determination that has brought him the success he has experienced in a book he wrote in 2016, titled *The Keys*. Name three other recording artists who have written and published a book; provide the name of the artists, the name of the book, and when it was published; and write a paragraph detailing the message presented in the book.

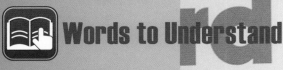
deduction: an amount removed or subtracted; with regard to taxes, an amount permitted to be subtracted from income earned so the amount that is subject to taxation is reduced.

dubbed: something that is named or given a new name or title; in movies, when the actors' voices have been replaced with those of different performers speaking another language; in music, transfer or copying of previously recorded audio material from one medium to another.

efficiency: measuring the point where the amount of work performed is either less than or equal to the amount of effort produced.

subsequently: something that takes place later or after some other event or action has taken place; the next thing in a sequence of events.

Chapter 4

Building DJ Khaled's Marketability

Venturing Outside Music

DJ Khaled's third album release, WE GLOBAL, led to his receiving BET's 2008 DJ of the Year Award. The attention he received as a result of that success led to his becoming the head of his first record label and being **dubbed** a music mogul.

Def Jam South

In the aftermath of his 2006 debut, DJ Khaled joined Def Jam South as president in 2008. The performer has set a new standard for artists, primarily as a deejay, with the ability to attract top artists in the industry. DJ Khaled **subsequently** moved from heading Def Jam Record's South label to creating his own label.

We the Best Music Group

We the Best Music Group was formed by DJ Khaled in 2008, around the time of the release of his third album. He uses the label as the main creative outlet for his

albums, working with other labels and distribution companies such as Universal Republic and Cash Money Entertainment, to name a few. All the collaborations he creates in the studio that end up on his albums go through We the Best Music Group.

Fashion

As mentioned, DJ Khaled bought into his fiancée's fashion line, ABU Apparels, in 2011. He also provides apparel through his We the Best label online and accessories that are in line with his brand.

Commercials and Endorsements

TurboTax

In 2017, DJ Khaled starred in a series of commercials for TurboTax tax software service. The 30-second spots feature him as a music industry mogul and entrepreneur seeking ways to maximize his tax **efficiency** and learn about the **deductions** he may have coming to him.

One such spot, released February 11, 2017, featured DJ Khaled hosting an exercise class while calling a support agent with TurboTax. He asks about the deductibility of his exercise equipment as a small-business owner.

Silk Original Soymilk

DJ Khaled has also done a series of commercials promoting the Silk Original Soymilk brand. A total of five spots have been recorded for the brand, including two ads that appeared on Snapchat and highlighted the benefits of making a Silk smoothie. One of the spots also featured tennis great Venus Williams.

Cîroc Mango

Another product DJ Khaled has featured prominently in commercials for is Cîroc, a mango-flavored vodka. In an October 2016 interview with *Billboard* magazine, he discussed how he became the face for Cîroc Mango.

Additional Commercials

The popular artist has also recorded ad spots for BET, Apple Music, Air Jordan, and cable and internet provider Comcast/XFINITY. He is a featured spokesperson for the brand of headphones offered by Dr. Dre/Apple's Beats by Dre. He has starred in several commercials for T Mobile's-sponsored BeatsX headphones, including several featuring performing artist Pharrell Williams.

Tackling the Small Screen

DJ Khaled has made various appearances on television and a cameo appearance in the movie *Pitch Perfect 3*. Here is a small sampling of some of his TV appearances.

The Four: Battle for Stardom

DJ Khaled is scheduled to appear as a judge and series regular in *The Four: Battle for Stardom*, a reality competition singing show appearing on the Fox Network. Hosted by singer Fergie, DJ Khaled will appear alongside rap mogul Sean Combs, pop star Meghan Trainor, and actor Charlie Walk. The show began airing on January 04, 2018.

The Ellen DeGeneres Show

March 09, 2016

DJ Khaled appeared on a season thirteen episode of *Ellen* in March 2016 as a guest, along with actors Felicity Huffman

Ellen DeGeneres

(*American Crime Story*) and Wendi McLendon-Covey (*Hello, My Name Is Doris*). It was the first time DJ Khaled appeared on the talk show.

Tom Hanks

September 09, 2016

DJ Khaled appeared on this season fourteen episode of *Ellen* as a musical guest, along with rapper Future. They performed the song *I've Got the Keys* from DJ Khaled's MAJOR KEYS album. Also appearing on the show was actor Tom Hanks, who was starring in *Scully* at the time.

November 21, 2016

Two months later, the artist again appeared on an episode of *Ellen* as a guest, along with actor Emma Stone *(La La Land)*. Martha Stewart and rapper Snoop Dogg also appeared on that episode, as well as singer Miley Cyrus.

Chelsea

May 25, 2016

DJ Khaled made an appearance in the seventh episode of the first season of Chelsea Handler's talk show, *Chelsea*. His appearance coincided with that of California's Senator Barbara Boxer.

July 27, 2016

DJ Khaled made a second appearance on Chelsea Handler's show, this time in episode thirty-one of the first season. He was joined on the show by Clay Aiken, Rachel Hoff, Jim Jefferies, Khloé Kardashian, Lisa Lampanelli, and NeNe Leakes.

Scan here to watch DJ Khaled with Ellen DeGeneres as a guest on *Ellen*

Jimmy Kimmel Live!

March 17, 2017

The hip-hop artist appeared as a guest on this episode of *Jimmy Kimmel Live!*, along with actors Tom Hiddleston *(Kong: Skull Island)* and Gillian Jacobs *(Love)*. Stand-up comedian Sam Jay also joined them.

Scan here to watch DJ Khaled discussing his new album, GRATEFUL, featuring Jay-Z and Beyoncé, with host Jimmy Kimmel

Scan here to watch DJ Khaled discussing one of his keys to success with host Stephen Colbert on *The Late Show*

The Late Show with Stephen Colbert

DJ Khaled made his debut appearance as a guest on *The Late Show with Stephen Colbert* in *The Late Show's* first season. Also appearing with host Stephen Colbert on this December 06, 2016, episode was Vice President Joe Biden.

RapFix Live

DJ Khaled sat down for a discussion with MTV personality Sway in *RapFix Live*, a show produced for the MTV network. Rap artist Juvenile accompanied him in this episode. DJ Khaled engaged in showing off his skills in some freestyle rap at the end of the program, alongside the other guests of this April 18, 2012, show.

The View

The midday show *The View* welcomed DJ Khaled as a guest on December 07, 2016. In this twentieth-season episode, he was interviewed by the panel, which consisted of Jedediah Bila, Joy Behar, Whoopi Goldberg, Sara Haines, and Sunny Hostin. He discussed his new book, *The Keys*.

Live! With Kelly

February 27, 2017

DJ Khaled served as the guest DJ in this special *LIVE's After Oscar Show*, along with guest co-host Ryan Seacrest and guest actor Jerry O'Connell and musical guest Flo Rida.

June 12, 2017

The hip-hop artist made another appearance on *Live!*

Scan here to watch DJ Khaled along with Juvenile performing a freestyle rap for the MTV show *RapFix Live*

Ryan Seacrest

With Kelly in this June 12, 2017, episode. Joining guest co-host Ryan Seacrest were actors Ethan Hawke and Tituss Burgess. DJ Khaled did not perform but dropped by the set with his son, Asahd.

Text-Dependent Questions:

❶ Who appeared as a guest in a December 06, 2016, episode of *The Late Show with Stephen Colbert* along with DJ Khaled?

❷ How many appearances has DJ Khaled made on *Jimmy Kimmel Live!*?

❸ What date did DJ Khaled first appear on the *Ellen DeGeneres Show*?

Research Project:

DJ Khaled was able to leverage the success of his third album release, WE GLOBAL, to not only be honored with BET's Best DJ Award but to also take over as president of the Def Jam South record label. He later went on to become the founder of his own label, We the Best Music Group. DJ Khaled is not the first artist to become the head of a music label (their own, or that of a major record label). Find three other examples of artists in the world of hip-hop who are currently the head (chairperson, CEO, and/or president) of their own recording label. Name the artist, the name of the label, and the year that the artist became the head "mogul" of the label.

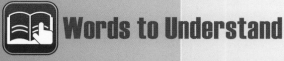

Words to Understand

ambassador: an individual who serves as an official representative of a person, country, or specific cause.

attain: to meet a goal or reach an accomplishment through personal effort.

enrich: to make better; to enhance a person's standing or situation through education, or some form of assistance.

espouse: to show support for a cause or a way of existence or life.

philosophy: a type of thought that defines how a person sees the world or how they see themselves in a world.

Some of DJ Khaled's Keys

DJ Khaled sees his role in life as **ambassador** of goodwill and success. He has come from a humble background, the child of immigrants who came to America to find a better life for their children. He has been exposed to opportunities that many people only dream of and has been introduced to individuals who have successfully advanced his career. This includes Cash Money's Birdman, Luke Skywalker, Fat Joe, and others.

In return, the deejay has gone out of his way to encourage newer and younger artists and give them a step up. *Holla at Me*, the lead single from DJ Khaled's first album, Listennn. . . the Album, also features Pitbull. Pitbull was virtually unknown at the time, but DJ Khaled wanted him. Not only

Pitbull

was he a good musician, but he represented the Miami club culture of the early 2000s.

Whenever he is given the opportunity, DJ Khaled likes to **espouse** his keys to success as explained in his book, *The Keys*. Some of his memorable quotes, which he has shared on Snapchat, provide further insight on how he stays focused and driven to success:

"LION!"—*No need to water down a Mufasa statue in your backyard. Just believe in the higher power.*

Sustenance is a major key to success—Even if it's a bowl of Cinnamon Toast Crunch and almond milk, or a turkey breakfast sandwich (Shout out to Chef Dee).

DJ Khaled, Asahd Tuck Khaled, his son and Nicole Tuck, his wife

Always take your best shot.

Massages are a weekly necessity—Especially when surrounded by bamboo and the sounds of the ocean.

Every conversation should begin with "This is off the record"—Even a call to your bestie.

Be a superstar—Even when they don't want you to.

Don't let anyone put time on you—It's always your time.

Dove soap and cocoa butter (no cologne) is the key—Staying fresh is so important for the culture.

Scan the code to watch DJ Khaled discussing, via Snapchat, one of his many keys to success—"LION!"

"In life, they have many directions; I choose to go up"— Always aim for the top.

"The key is to make it"— Whether lost at sea on a jet ski or your own personal journey, always have faith.

It is important to understand that the musician's keys drive the support he gives to the industry that has done so much for him, both personally and professionally. His keys are also the underlying **philosophy** that motivates him to do good acts and set a good example for his son, his family, and his community.

Charitable activities that DJ Khaled has been involved in include:

- Global Fund to Fight AIDS, Tuberculosis and Malaria, an international financing organization that raises money to prevent and treat those diseases

- (RED), based in Geneva, Switzerland and formed by U2 singer Bono; this initiative raises awareness and funds to help eliminate HIV/AIDS in eight African countries

- i.am.angel Foundation (Wauwatosa, Wisconsin), founded by former Black Eyed Peas singer will.i.am; the organization works on educational opportunities for youth

Personal Contributions

On September 20, 2013, DJ Khaled teamed up with radio station Hot 99 Jamz to give $10,000 to the band and music program at Miami's Norland High School.

Get Schooled Fashion Benefit

DJ Khaled's signature look, expressed in his suits, sweat suits, and other types of clothing apparel, became the subject of an auction for a good cause. DJ Khaled teamed up with the online social marketplace for fashion, Poshmark.com, for the event, which was to benefit the nonprofit organization Get Schooled. The auction of his personal apparel took place in July and August of 2017, with a portion of the funds donated to the Win More Music campaign, through the nonprofit Get Schooled.

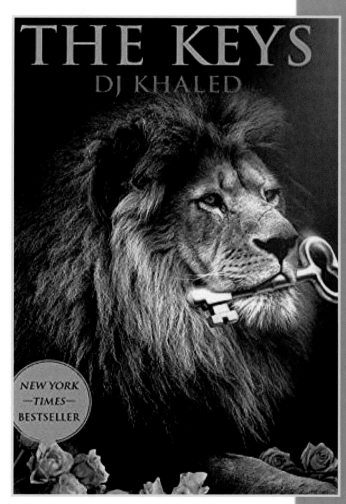

Win More Music

This initiative, which is a partnership between DJ Khaled and Get Schooled, is an effort to engage middle school and high school students and guide them toward careers in the music industry. Students' involvement in the program allows them access to DJ Khaled's keys and provides their schools with equipment and support to keep music programs alive. In turn, that provides a creative outlet for students to express themselves.

The program not only focuses on how music can **enrich** the lives of students and guide them on the path toward success, it also identifies seven specific keys to success that students can strive to incorporate. These keys are in the areas of healthy living and lifestyles, financial literacy, and making better choices.

During the 2016–2017 school year, students participating in the campaign found that the process of setting goals and **attaining** a key did the following:

- "Gave them good information": 75 percent

- Encouraged them to "think big": 57 percent

- Helped them set goals: 70 percent

- Helped them get smarter at managing money: 55 percent

- Helped them make better decisions: 60 percent

- Helped them set themselves up for success: 64 percent

Conclusion

DJ Khaled's life came from humble beginnings in New Orleans, Louisiana. His parents' love of music influenced his career choice. Through his efforts and hard work, he was able to put himself in position to be one of the best deejays in hip-hop today, as well as a studio executive and recognized talent.

The musician's road to success is, at best, not the traditional route that other entertainers have taken, but there is not a lot about him that seems to meet the definition of "traditional." He easily laughs at himself, even when faced with a tough situation—like being lost in the ocean on a jet ski—but manages to reach for a key to drive him toward success and personal growth.

The future for DJ Khaled, his fiancée Nicole Tuck, and their son Asahd appears to be bright, and as long as he maintains his positive outlook and large store of ambition and drive, there's no telling how far this shooting star of hip-hop will rise!

Text-Dependent Questions:

❶ What percentage of students participating in DJ Khaled's Win More Music campaign claimed that completing one key provided them with good information?

❷ In what months of 2017 did DJ Khaled participate in an auction of his clothes to benefit the Win More Music campaign?

❸ What nonprofit did DJ Khaled partner with in 2017 to provide opportunities for middle and high school students?

Research Project:

DJ Khaled's partnership with the Win More Music campaign was a charitable effort that he felt was important as part of his determination to give back to the community, and to young people in particular. What are some other examples of efforts by hip-hop artists to give back directly to school-aged children to inspire them to become successful? Name at least two such efforts, the artist involved, and the types of results that have been obtained.

Series Glossary of Key Terms

A&R: an abbreviation that stands for Artists and Repertoire, which is a record company department responsible for the recruitment and development of talent; similar to a talent scout for sports.

ambient: a musical style that relies on electronic sounds, gentle music, and the lack of a regular beat to create a relaxed mood for the listener.

brand: a particular product or a characteristic that serves to identify a particular product; a brand name is one having a well-known and usually highly regarded or marketable word or phrase.

cameo: also called a cameo role; a minor part played by a prominent performer in a single scene of a motion picture or a television show.

choreography: the art of planning and arranging the movements, steps, and patterns of dancers.

collaboration: a product created by working with someone else; combining individual talents.

debut: a first public appearance on a stage, on television, or so on, or the beginning of a profession or career; the first appearance of something, like a new product.

deejay (DJ): a slang term for a person who spins vinyl records on a turntable; aka a disc jockey.

demo: a recording of a new song, or of one performed by an unknown singer or group, distributed to disc jockeys, recording companies, and the like, to demonstrate the merits of the song or performer.

dubbed: something that is named or given a new name or title; in movies, when the actors' voices have been replaced with those of different performers speaking another language; in music, transfer or copying of previously recorded audio material from one medium to another.

endorsement: money earned from a product recommendation, typically by a celebrity, athlete, or other public figure.

entrepreneur: a person who organizes and manages any enterprise, especially a business, usually with considerable initiative and at financial risk.

falsetto: a man singing in an unnaturally high voice, accomplished by creating a vibration at the very edge of the vocal chords.

genre: a subgroup or category within a classification, typically associated with works of art, such as music or literature.

hone, honing: sharpening or refining a set of skills necessary to achieve success or perform a specific task.

icon: a symbol that represents something, such as a team, a religious person, a location, or an idea.

innovation: the introduction of something new or different; a brand-new feature or upgrade to an existing idea, method, or item.

instrumental: serving as a crucial means, agent, or tool; of, relating to, or done with an instrument or tool.

jingle: a short verse, tune, or slogan used in advertising to make a product easily remembered.

mogul: someone considered to be very important, powerful, and in charge; a term usually associated with heads of businesses in the television, movie studio, or recording industries.

performing arts: skills that require public performance, as acting, singing, or dancing.

philanthropy: goodwill to fellow members of the human race; an active effort to promote human welfare.

public relations: the activity or job of providing information about a particular person or organization to the public so that people will regard that person or organization in a favorable way.

sampler: a digital or electronic musical instrument, related to a synthesizer, that uses samples, or sound recordings, of real instruments (trumpet, violin, piano, etc.) mixed with excerpts of recorded songs and other interesting sounds (sirens, ocean waves, construction noises, car horns, etc.) that are stored digitally and can be replayed by a triggering device, like a sequencer, electronic drums, or a MIDI keyboard.

single: a music recording having two or more tracks that is shorter than an album, EP, or LP; also, a song that is particularly popular, independent of other songs on the same album or by the same artist.

Citations

". . . fist-pumping song cycle of triumph in the hood," by David Jeffries. "DJ Khaled: Victory/AllMusic Review by David Jeffries." AllMusic.com.

"lockerz.com/s/204681889 I'm sry I couldn't. . . " by DJ Khaled. Diep, Eric. "DJ Khaled's Tour Bus Explodes before Concert in Florida." Complex.com. April 29, 2012.

". . . cause that's my brother. . . " by DJ Khaled. Kramer, Kyle. "DJ Khaled's First Hit Featured Lil Wayne, Paul Wall, Fat Joe, Pitbull, and Rick Ross." *DJ Booth*. July 13, 2017.

". . . a Fat Joe on steroids," by Fat Joe. Clayton, Jayce. "How DJ Khaled Won Friends, Money, and Power." *The Fader*. June 12, 2013.

". . . anthem king of hip-hop. . . " by Keith Murphy. Murphy, Keith. "Khaled: Behind the Scenes with Hip-Hop's Anthem King." Billboard.com. June 06, 2011.

". . . dubbed the "King of Snapchat. . . " CNBC.com. Castillo, Michelle. "'King of Snapchat' DJ Khaled Explains How to Succeed on Social Media." June 15, 2017.

"What's so beautiful about life. . . " by DJ Khaled. Shanahan, Mark. "DJ Khaled Speaks to Harvard Business School Students." BostonGlobe.com. December 13, 2016.

"Well, 'The Keys,' man, is the keys to success. . . " by DJ Khaled. NPR staff. "DJ Khaled Throws Us the Keys." NPR. January 06, 2017.

"The key is to make it. . . Perseverance at sea," by DJ Khaled. Mench, Chris. "DJ Khaled Got Lost at Sea and Snapchatted the Whole Experience." Complex.com. December 14, 2015.

"Gave them good information. . . Think Big. . . " Get Schooled website. [n.d.]

Further Reading

Coogan, Nancy. *DJ Khaled Major Key Lyrics*. CreateSpace Independent Publishing Platform, 2016.

Coval, Kevin, Lansana, Quraysh Ali, and Marshall, Nate. *The BreakBeat Poets: New American Poetry in the Age of Hip-Hop*. Chicago: Haymarket Books, 2015.

Katz, Mark. *Groove Music: The Art and Culture of the Hip-Hop DJ.* Bethesda, MD: Oxford University Press, 2012.

Khaled, DJ. *The Keys*. New York: Crown/Archetype, 2016.

Meseke, Mitch. *The Illustrated Guide to Hip-Hop A–Z*. Independently published, 2017.

Miller, Matt. *Bounce: Rap Music and Local Identity in New Orleans.* Amherst, MA: University of Massachusetts Press, 2012.

Ridenhour, Carlton Douglas ("Chuck D"). *This Day in Rap and Hip-Hop History*. London: Octopus, 2017.

Sirois, Andre. *Hip Hop DJs and the Evolution of Technology*. New York: Peter Lang, 2012.

Internet Resources

www.billboard.com
The official site of Billboard Music, with articles about artists, chart information, and more.

www.thefader.com/
Official website for a popular New York City–based music magazine.

www.hiphopweekly.com
A young adult hip-hop magazine.

thesource.com/
Website for a bimonthly magazine that covers hip-hop and pop culture.

www.vibe.com/
Music and entertainment website and a member of Billboard Music, a division of Billboardwx-Hollywood Reporter Media Group.

wethebeststore.com/
DJ Khaled's official website for his record label, We the Best Music Group.

Educational Videos

Chapter 1:
http://x-qr.net/1GdW
http://x-qr.net/1H7o
http://x-qr.net/1GdB
http://x-qr.net/1FfC
http://x-qr.net/1FiN
http://x-qr.net/1EKe
http://x-qr.net/1DfT
http://x-qr.net/1H0g
http://x-qr.net/1DuM

Chapter3:
http://x-qr.net/1HRJ
http://x-qr.net/1FUr

Chapter4:
http://x-qr.net/1GKy
http://x-qr.net/1DDf
http://x-qr.net/1Cxr
http://x-qr.net/1FCK

Chapter5:
http://x-qr.net/1FbB

Photo Credits

Chapter 1:
ID 23301392 © Laurence Agron | Dreamstime
ID 24305521 © Carrienelson1 | Dreamstime
ID 24618180 © Sbukley | Dreamstime
ID 47646025 © Dwong19 | Dreamstime
ID 74169164 © Lu Yang | Dreamstime
ID 80952286 © Starstock | Dreamstime
DU-lf_jU0AAUc5X.jpg | Flickr
RD Whittington Ray J &DJ KHALID.jpg | Flickr
31001984312_4e08daf4c1_b.jpg | Flikr
Chance_The_Rapper_2013.jpg | Wikimedia Creative Commons
DJ_Khaled_2012.jpg | Meghan Roberts | Wikimedia Commons

Chapter 2:
ID 33286755 © Randy Miramontez | Dreamstime
ID 65957819 © Emevil | Dreamstime
ID 83989201 © Frui | Dreamstime
ID 88173026 © Starstock | Dreamstime
ID 98899627 © Starstock | Dreamstime

Chapter 3:
BeyAccept.jpg | YouTube
ID 27559790 © Roystudio | Dreamstime
ID 34073910 © Little_prince | Dreamstime
ID 40376944 © Abdullatif Omar | Dreamstime
ID 72777250 © Kobby Dagan | Dreamstime
ID 81361283 © Starstock | Dreamstime
ID 85366920 © Wdnetagency | Dreamstime
ID 35296249 © Ivan Mikhaylov | Dreamstime

Chapter 4:
ID 26491511 © Featureflash | Dreamstime
ID 31065112 © Laurence Agron | Dreamstime
ID 32458252 © Carrienelson1 | Dreamstime
ID 81357238 © Starstock | Dreamstime
37112883505_4bdbbbf16c_o.jpg | Flikr
37818545154_cd183856a4_o.jpg | Flikr

Chapter 5:
ID 10303403 © Fred Rike | Dreamstime
ID 17095991 © Ken Woods | Dreamstime
ID 38421348 © Pixelrobot | Dreamstime
ID 24305506 © Carrienelson1 | Dreamstime
30324397964_af5fa0b30d_o.jpg | Flikr
31148589495_84d2c2a7c5_b.jpg | Flikr
32850454465_c4066b1d7c_o.jpg | Flikr
36970229901_f73886cda8_o.jpg | Flikr
37111673955_31edf23731_o.jpg | Flikr
37818545154_cd183856a4_o.jpg | Flikr
38476137866_a88ec4efe7_o.jpg | Flikr
ID 35590456 © 2day929 | Dreamstime.com

Index

DJ Khaled
HIP-HOP & R&B

Index

Index

Index

Author's Biography

Joe L. Morgan is a father, author, and budding saxophonist. A music enthusiast all of his life, he shares his love of every type of music with his children, family, and friends, from modern jazz to dance and hip-hop.